Face Value

The apparition of these faces in the crowd;
Petals on a wet, black bough.

—Ezra Pound

to Robert Tucker of Amherst,
the Teacher,
and my friend in poetry for twenty years.

F.T.U. Contemporary Poetry Series

A Florida Technological University Book

Orlando / 1977

The University Presses of Florida

FACE
VALUE

EDMUND
SKELLINGS

"Heartwood" and "Friendly Game" first appeared in *Monument* (Arizona State).

"Leavings" appeared in *Midwestern University Quarterly*.

"Welfare Shout" first appeared in *Florida Quarterly*.

"Strangling," "Artistic," and "Librarian" appeared in *Fireland Arts Review* (Bowling Green).

"Warning to the Earth" appeared first in *New Poetry* (Australia).

"Melodramatics" appeared in *Bridge*.

"A Needle's Eye" appeared first in *West of Boston* (anthology).

"To a Beauty" appeared in *Metamorphosis*.

"Creative Writing Notebook" first appeared in *In The Poet's Hand* (anthology: Maryland Library Association).

"For a Friend with Two Years to Live" and "Specialist Ad Vice" appeared in *Gryphon*.

"The Tracks of Tyros" appeared in *Lillabulero*.

"Children's Verse" appeared first in *The Miami Herald*.

"How to Pick a Mistress, Or" and "Understanding is a Tone of Voice Blues" appeared in *The South Florida Review*.

"Sharpy" and "Owner" appeared first in *The Chinese Student Weekly* (Hong Kong).

"Projection" appeared in *The Iowa Defender*.

printed in florida

Library of Congress Cataloging in Publication Data

Skellings, Edmund.
  Face value.

  Poems.
  "A Florida Technological University book."
  I. Title.
PS3537.K33F3   811'.5'4   77–24634
ISBN 0–8130–0594–9

Contents

780739

Face Value

Opening Shock

One is never prepared for it:
Although you clench the whole body
And even count the seconds off,
Whacko! Who would think silken cloth
Could stop you in midair so hard, so
Sudden is the word, like bone
Popping. And it can take the heels
From the boots, watch from the wrist,
Zippo through the pocket bottom.
But we never cursed the old T-Seven.
Laughter as it let us down from heaven.

It's natural as being born, our sergeant
Wise cracked, checking the umbilicals.
See, I remember each and every detail.
No STEP, stenciled the wing in warning.

God.   Was the sky *blue* that morning.

Dass Ich Erkenne

Yes, it's your old Whether
Man again, Ed Skellings
Here. Only poet writes
With both hands, folks,
Only poet with no poem about
Mirrors. But

Rectification is at *hand*,
Chillun, is at
Hand. Now

Consider your average electron
Trapped by powerful magnets
And levitated, yes,
I said *levitated*
In an energy well. Well,

Nick that little charged
Particle with a microwave,
Nick one direction, nick
The other, measure gently
La difference, and voilà

One has this measurement.

And if, which is where the
Whether comes in,
I say and if
One uses the positron
For a quick comparison,

Well! We all will see
If matter and antimatter
Are exact mirror images
Exactly. And if not

Oh oh. If explodes,

Whether evaporates,
Metaphor won't and
Bye bye Aristotle.

Tectonic

Damned town is mined,
They mutter in Cumberland.
Most all Maryland balances
On worms of tunnels.

Come long hot summers,
Fairbanks will sink
Through the permafrost,
Spits the sourdough.

And at Miami, adds a cane,
The sea seeps salt
As we suck up fresh. Tap
Tap. Shaky Frisco!

We grow disturbed
For a moment, sit
And muse a minute.
But then we settle,

Forget what volcanos
Murmur, mumble, bubble
Over hell ever under.
Pave away, bulldozer,

Path to a further city:
We'll get the wig rewoven,
Not hear the heart's trouble,
Ignore news from the bone.

Extra Extra

I just found out Richard Nixon
Made TV commercials selling himself
Paid for by Abplanalp's money
Which Abplanalp made from royalties
On his patented aerosol valve
Which is obsolete because of the ozone.

On top of that this late president
Appeared on millions of TV screens
Once again selling himself but now
To the whole world as he stepped
Up onto the Great China Wall.

And at that identical moment
Another large cash contributor
Named Howard Hughes was hiding
In a penthouse suite in Nicaragua
While Nixon was carried live
By the Hughes TV network.

And now I suppose you are angry
With me because this poem doesn't
Rhyme or have a moral.

Bicentennial History Lesson

Adolph was dissatisfied. He ordered
The priceless Gobelin tapestries
Torn down. In the last bunker
All walls would be raw concrete.
Waving his Walther, he directed
The removal of the final vestige
Of ostentation. Eva came then,
And the two of them settled in.

When Churchill slipped away
From the meeting on a whim
To visit Berlin (waiting for Joe
Stalin's slow train to cross Poland)
Winston stopped at the top step,
Then descended almost one flight,
Then slowly came back up out
From the bunker. His aides
Found three iron crosses,
Took two broken pieces of marble
Tabletop, and one torn paper
Scrap of the wall map of the world.

Even Harry Truman couldn't
Resist, and he slipped away,
Too, and his Chrysler convertible
Crossed and re-crossed the path
Of Churchill's Rolls-Royce
As they took the same expensive
Tour. His aides pocketed two
Iron crosses and three marble
Chunks big as a fist to use,
Back home, as paper weights.
That day, back home, in New
Mexico, a bomb had gone largely off.

That day, on the other
Side of the round world,
The Emperor sat imperially alone,
Defying generations of custom,
Awaiting the Prince to whom
He would order surrender.

Now you know what I know.
Some of us are less, some more
Than two hundred years old.

1976 Florida Almanac

With fourteen deepwater ports
Florida is unequalled in facilities
For water transportation, says
The almanac, as if everyone didn't know.

One does find out things, though,
About the number of
Surgical-Medical Misadventures:
Seventy-three. And that two died
Of high and low air pressure,
Probably one each. Did you know
The California Poppy blooms
March to June, is hardy,
Re-seeds and volunteers readily?

Four hundred eighty-eight persons
Dropped dead in unspecified falls
From unspecified heights, pushed
By no one specified. Think of that.

The Tangelo is a hybrid, naturally,
And its orange-tangerine
Only really good for out-of-hand eating.

Florida has all the necessary
Ingredients for cement, imagine.
And all United States production
Of staurolite is confined here.
No diamonds we know of. Large
Quantities of gold off shore.
Forged in pieces of eight.

No American Indians were
Expelled from school in any county
During the whole of Nineteen Seventy-Three.
How exemplary.

Murder statistics are in the back
For obvious reasons. Everyone
Has something to hide, but
Twenty-three under the age of five?
And increasing? Your average felon was
Twenty-four, Baptist, came
From a broken home, was
Occupationally unskilled, had
No priors, got four years.

The University of Florida plays There
Home Home There Home There There.
The University of Miami simply plays.

And if everything runs true in '76
The hounds will run at Flagler,
The horses at Gulfstream Park.
Six hundred and fourteen people will drown.
Fifty-seven inches of rain will
Fall in Dade County.

Raccoon, beaver, bobcat, Key Largo
Wood rats, and all reptiles
Other than alligator will go
Once again, unprotected.

The state will go Democratic.
The beaches will continue to erode.

Alaska

I suppose it was the picture of Frenchie,
Toothless grin, leaning on the big radial
Engine of the Cessna with the broken prop,
Broken ski, shack in the background,
Rusted oil drums scattered everywhere,
I suppose it was the picture of Frenchie,

But I have tossed aside the book on politics
And I am flying once more in the Bush
Past that huge white rock of the sky
That the Eskimo call The Great One,
And I skid down again at Talkeetna
To drink hot coffee in the one cafe.

I suppose it was the picture of Frenchie,
Long lost by the time I found him,
A photo in a flight shed in Nenana,
That moved into my mind while reading
Out of doors in the perfumes of Florida.
I suppose it was the picture of Frenchie.

On The Death Of Your Father

for Glenn Goerke

Birth and death share the same
Smell, Glenn, you said,
Looking for some
Simile, some
Comparison, some
Way of making the thing clear.

My friend. There is no
Way. Nothing will ever be
The same. Death
Is definition.

Adams, Jefferson, those great
Fathers died on this day.
Who can think on them? Personal
Grief flares like a rocket. We feel
The house divided.

We say, thank heaven he
Suffers no longer. Finally,
We sigh, it is over.

We know a lie, having lied
Before. This is a lie.
We taste even a good lie
On our lips. Truth is

He should have gone on forever.
And we should go on forever,
Let all else lapse.

Outside, a nation's fireworks
Explode, proclaiming
Celebrations of our liberty.

You and I know we live in chains
Of flesh. Liberty is for a time
And in a place. Birth and death
Have no smell. They are words
For the living.

History clamors for another man,
Hungering, unsatisfied,
Another man, another man.

Let fools try to console you.
They have always known
What is essential and necessary.

But listen to my poem whisper,

Our bones make the past real.

Male Lead

for Burt Reynolds

They make you who you never thought you'd be.
And then they fall in love with it.

No telling who you might have really been.
Or still might be.

You work becoming someone else
With the care and delicacy of a spy.
Learning your lines, you mutter
To whatever self you are today,
Let me see now. Where was I?

You play a king.
And each night are dethroned.

Each night, like a real cop,
Turn in your badge.

Tomorrow all the action scenes:
The fight, the roof, the long chase
Down the clanging fire escape.

Much later some director
Will edit your imitation life together.

You watch a hand performing autographs.
Which role is signing this year?

14

You are your own talk show host
And deadpan to the mirror,
Be Yourself!

Alone, no one is Hero. No one The Lover.

The world still snarls in its toughest way,
Get this straight.

And always the hidden writer sighing,

Say after me. Say after me.

Radio John

for John Eastman and WIOD Miami

Your voice is dark as the night
We listen in.

One o'clock is always hungry
For company. And for many
And for more each year
That black phone is the only wire
To anyone.

Ring me, ring me, ring me,
Goes the bell. John,
You're always there.

We'll talk of love long distance
And at night time rates.

We'll tell the time of our lives
And how we almost drowned in it.

We'll chat of hate, we'll
Listen in on others
Who give themselves away.

We'll say (but softly to ourselves)
That guy makes sense.
That lady is a nut.
That poor man needs a friend so bad
He makes me *mad*.

You name the tune. We'll sing
Of anything beneath the sun.
Or moon. We'll tattletale
All secrets but our names.

John, John, do you recognize
My voice?
I feel like I have spent my life
Hanging on.

Timer

Hello, I am expired again
For want of a silver dime.

In Iowa City once
The local junkie, Lonesome,
Leaning on a meter, said, Man,
It's all
When the time runs out.

It did. His last letter
From the institution asked
Money to publish
His numerical analysis
Of History.

George, I still count syllables.
My moment, too, is almost up.
The centers of our downtowns scream

Red Flag! Red Flag!

Violations abound. Stay
Mad. I will buy,
And think of you,
A cherry Cadillac, park
Anywhere I want.

Vitamin

Mr. J.C. (53) of Damascus, Arkansas,
Had an enlarged heart, bad valves, poor
Circulation before taking vitamin E.

He reports: "The heart size is reduced,
My circulation and breathing are better
And I have less fainting and few leg cramps."

All that we are happy to know, although
The better off will smile and turn the page,
The worse will be jealous at your improvement.

And though I can see you holding your calf
While the tears pour down until you fall
On the worn carpet in the front room of your house,
My poem is not looking for clear image or moral.

Enough that you never know I write of my heart
That each year it seems both larger and weaker
And therefore my circulation is poorer
For no remedy helps me to get around.

THREE AROUND THE
YOUNG GENTLEMAN

Way Out On The Way Out

for John Berryman

You must think I'm blind
You push your words in
Till my hands turn red from the wringing
Knuckles all cracked

In fact

My future swells from your grip
Life line slap like a whip
Touch deafen numb and tear

Assur ed
When you join the dead
Body will twitch till the sun set

And mine will too mon brer

Ends

for John Berryman

"Zany enlivens."

Well so. If one palavers past
The grave, I
Can talk to you done John.
Figure you under water.
You always wanted to get to what
Scrawled the skin on the scrotum, ah, us,
Inflected and gendered, oh,
Well so, the day I heard you
Suicided, I felt like
John Berryman.
Another John dead dog gone on,
How
Does every dear John oh God go
Sass
In nation?

On Falling

for John Berryman

The winds are old, have all
Been breathed by someone,
Sung by a few. I, too,
Laid myself out on the air,
Felt not me fall,
But the great ground rush up,

Big mother kiss, big
Belly whopper.

Every poem, John, is jus
Playing for Time.

What's Mine

My cat makes me laugh.
We are in the dark together,
See, and I say to him,
You are bad as Robert Frost,
Yowling about fences. You are.

Suppose the blue Maltese
Does cross each night
Yard to yard, hedging along,
Belly on the earth, maybe
It's only a shortcut home
To his own bowl of fish,
His own kitchen heaven.

I should buy the place
Next door, I suppose?
Put up a sign keeping out
All cats of a differing stripe?

Let live, I shout from the pool.
And how many times have I told you,
Don't claw the screen!

For A Friend With Two Years To Live

She walks in a world where everything is known.
And as if the colors in her clothes were braille
Her fingers fret the textures.

Now she tells us of a climb
Upon a ridge not far from here,
The cold rock seeping through her skirt
As she picked her sweater free from burrs.

Alerted to the lightest touch,
Our fingers prickle feeling how
We pluck to keep our own warmth pure.

And so her listeners begin the climb.
We breathe a bit more heavily. We sit.
And we can almost feel our eyes
Tear from the chilly wind.

Heartwood

You chopped the tree down though it held my house
And tore away the brush and cleared a court.
Too young to play, I loved to watch the sport,
So if it cost my house I felt no loss.

From a rickety ladder at net height
The ball was like my globe at school, but white.
I didn't know the rules. It was my game
To see who kept the ball longest in air,
Patting my leather world with his strong hands.
But when it stayed so long I thought it tame,
Someone would slip and miss it bouncing, or
Somebody near the net would thump it down.

Then the turtle came. And volleyball
Raised no more dust in air than catching him.
Two feet across, at least six inches tall,
He eyed the ring of feet, looked for a place to swim,
And finding none, pulled in his legs and tail.
The head stayed part way out. His leather back
Was brown, but stitched and round, like half the ball.

"Ride 'im, Romey!" And for a little while
You, father, stood astride half of my globe,
Taller than everyone. O, what a smile!

"There is a story that if you set flame
Beneath a turtle's belly he will crawl
Out of his shell," one of the big men said.
"I wonder if he would?" "Can't ever tell!"

You carried oily rags from the garage
And rolled the turtle on them with a stick
And once it was begun the test was quick.
A match was struck, and caught in seas of fire
The turtle tried to dig down to his mud.

Whoever told the story was a liar.

A summer of scrapes, and bitter bruises, too.
Always your voice to flinch me, "You won't die!"
So I did all a boy can ever do.
I ran away from laughing gods to cry.

It was a wicked summer I recall.
More than a turtle died within his shell
The day house tree and legend fell.

Leavings

It stuns like being present
At the massacre of myself
To turn so at the doorway
And see sprawled on the sofa
My mangled twisted clothing.

Crucified in woolen,
My bent and crippled arms
Torture all composure
And there my severed ankles
Rest in separate leathers.

The vision forces thought
To tear from a frightened past
Red seconds in a war
When all were scattered silly
And frozen in odd forms

And then to nearer losses,
A first wife and father,
Vanished now for years,
And how I feel the traces
In their personal effects.

I pick up this silk tie
Much as a lover might,
Upon discovering absence,
And hold it to my cheek
To cool the bloody skin.

For fondling these close things
Is tenderness making believe
That I have truly gone
And now that I have known
This night, I truly have.

Shorelines

Root of my hair,
Oasis,

I can feel the bottom of you,
Wet with shade.

Nail of my hand, your
Mandarin flick, your
Grub for worms.

Was I the only child
To lift my father's delicate cold
Fearsome eyelid

And look at the nothing
Behind me

And the nothing ahead?

Root of my life,
Atom,
Founding vibration,
What have you washed up?

Folklore

Invariably I look back for help.
In one of my early poems a man
With the world on his hands stands
On the back of a huge turtle.

Those Greeks could tell a myth.
Today I learned the Turkish earth
Is held on the horns of an ox.
Earthquakes when his head shakes.

What story shall we tell
Our children born in our Hell?
Something is obviously shaking
Its head. Some back is breaking.

The Distrophy Of Certain Muscles

It is usually without warning
Just when we have our guard down
So this morning
While we were dreaming
In fragrant lathers, crisp neckerchieves,
Towels steaming,

Into the glare of mirrors they wheeled you,
Everyone more than ordinarily fussy,
And from a mechanical chair
Lifted you and arranged you
In a mechanical chair.
Then they adjusted it.

Grotesque ideas were born:
What style could you possibly wish?
Would they hold up a mirror and ask
Do you approve?

Or would they take a crazy glass
To make you see your form
Straight as a razor,
Tall as a barber,
Smooth as a Lucky Tiger.

We could all bolt upright,
Stagger outside like bloody Caesars
Crying ruin, weeping betrayal.
Unpinned,
We could fall apart at the seams.

But the scissors
Snicker.
Our hair gets thinned.
The ritual keeps us disciplined.

Friendly Game

So. You're blind. Well, that's the way with war.
No man comes back the one he was before.
As you come tapping toward me on the street,
My mind feels back to where the boys would meet.

Up went the hoop behind O'Neill's garage
And soon the grass was scuffed and dribbled from
A round bare spot of ground where boys could dodge
Their suppers to play basketball. And come
The time of choosing up, the first pick took
You always on his team. You were the best
For neighborhoods around, and wore a look
That said your play with us was half in jest.

You scorned backboards. The idea was to win
With handicap, agility and grin.
Rebounds fell into your hands. The sets
You threw wore out imaginary nets,
And we heard future coliseums roar
As those shots fell to swell the final score.
A lot of guys just played to get a tan.
Why did I always face you for my man?

Has no one ever noticed your slight smile,
As if you heard a cheering from the past?
As you go by, my hand, in the old style,
Twitches a shot. I fake you out at last.

Monarch

It fluttered in the fallen leaves.
The cat put out one paw to bring
Up a butterfly with a torn wing.

Tom had one hind leg crippled
When he was young and fought.
I can imagine what he thought.

Fairbanks, Alaska

The white house belongs to Leo Hardy.
Eight years ago his wife gassed herself.
The fact that it was a Florence Range
Stuck in the family memory
For no reason.

The two sons married and had girls.
And when the older, Martin, was twenty-nine,
He went out to the dark garage
And stuffed its broken windows.
Then he started the engine of his car.

Above the mailbox that reads Leo Hardy,
Above the long back stairsteps of the white house,
Windbells hang,
Though, in the Interior, wind is rare.

Today the black crows are soaring
Near the white house
And the glass bells make clear notes
That carry.

Louise Is From Iowa

She is plain.
And natural.
And her forehead is fair.
Through the grain of her hair
One can hear the midwest rustle.
That is not important today, for

This last year she has taken to laughing
With a slight reservation of breath,
The first nuance of an autumn.
And the fur on my bones rustles.

Rarely, but more often, and now,
She looks up at me like an earth
I have bladed part of my life upon.
And her eyes are brown open wounds.

So Lonely In Hartford

for Wallace Stevens

Well Wallace, there is me and you now.
And that glass of water.

Bet you thought no one would find you,
Bet you paid premiums.

Maybe even guessed
Someone would add booze
Or get seasick one.

Not though do a figure eight near the brim.
Tip his tam to you goin past on one foot.

Or sit on the safedge, cast a mean fly,
Bring a girl down to be alone.

Bet you thought it was your pool.
Put up a po em to keep out the riff raff.

Well Wallace,
Never forgive you Wallace,
So lonely in Hartford,
And how you had to spell it out near the end.

Children's Verse

for Debra Segal

She is coming towards me on wooden legs
All right
Is Debra

Exactly as explained in the pathetic newspapers
Iterated in black and white nitrate

Forget the poetry
Each of my practiced feelings is a failure
She looks up out of a crippled vision
Scarcely under control

Oh

Behind her twisted smile
Thousands of manhours of motherlove
And fatherfear

Staggering steps

Debra crutches toward us past the delicate china
Past . . .
And the expensive furniture rugs tapestries
Turn to a linen lace
The air is scented with concern
Debra is

We hold our breaths afraid to even
Smell perhaps each others fright
What are the others thinking
Debra is walking

Fear of all the bad dreams now

Debra is stepping smiling towards us

In our living room

Whose reach exceeds yes her
Frightening so trustful
Grasp

Librarian

Yes yes she knew it.
Here even,
In the thinnest of positions,
Where only competence was required,

Error has multiplied.
Surface has been flawed
Like a bitten yellow pencil
Used only to express
Nerves.

She pats a stray dry curl
And another ravels from its clip.
Glasses dangle at the end of their chain
As she rubs the bridge of her nose.

The library is quiet.
Very quiet.
Tomorrow she will pick up her check
With exactly that silence.

Behind her
The books sing and sing.

Artistic

He could hear music blow
Toward and away,
Waver right and left.

No wonder
Dogs barked.

He saw paintings as heavy
Or light.
Imagined the hairs drag in the pigment,
Palette knife plaster the canvas
No wonder
Friends laughed.

One day he hung himself up
For all to view.

Only Eyes

Rainy day driving
And the wiperbeat wiperbeat wiperbeat

Fancies of a wife dead
And another girl other girl

And a daughter dead and a mother
Other no other no other

Watchout wiperbeat lonely eyes

Specialty

Glottochronology is my favorite
Science, though you've never heard
About it. Men trained in this
Study how words distort as time
Passes, how the tongue muscles
Itself, how the bones change
As a result of meaning shifting,

How the face finally expresses.

It would seem evolution favors
More and more communication
And very slowly and I mean
Very slowly all of us poets
Are having a visible impact.

I am half in love with
Iambic pentameter myself
Because I like the way tongues
Flap flap. Something sensual
There. But I can do
Without it. And sometimes

Without how your lips got that way.

Advertising

The front of your brain is blue.
Green in some lights.
Back of that, I am told,
All is grey.
And is so for everyone.

Which should do to make suspect
All who claim colorful
Dreams, schemes, personalities,
Anything made of idea.

You. Keep up the good front.

Likeness

The birds on those telephone wires
Perch like notes on a staff.
They bear an obvious resemblance,
But at this moment are quiet as a book.

My wife often takes out her music
And soon little birds punctuate the air.
I hear each typewriter key from another,
Though I admit deeper strains fill my head.

What if everything we saw came together
And the surf of the clouds and the waves
Ran off the wet page of the maestro
And he couldn't continue for his tears?

Flying Circus

On the road the dry leaves clown.
Summer's blue tarpaulin's down.
Frost has slackened the pennant vines
And struck the scarlet climber's lines.
Meadow-wide, the spendthrift trees
Have frittered away their currencies.

The last act of a summer run
Plays to a standing house of one:
Barnstorming butterflies sweep past;
A cricket band in the brush has massed;
Locusts sway on their stems with grace;
A spider sets her net. In case.

Seasoned performers, I catch breath
At this cool disregard of death,
And though, aloof, you never pause,
Acknowledging my brisk applause,
I number in your staunch supporters.
Daredevils, where are your winter quarters?

—1958

A Dark Outline

The dentist held up those odd shadows
So that over the years
I could see how things were going.

My hand for example shad*ed* this page.
ed stuck out under the index finger.
Thanks yet none of the bones were showing.

Nails manicured in Miami,
Palm discovered in Alaska,
Sperm walking San Francisco,

Soon I will go into the globe in a slow flowing,
Leaving only this poem glowing.

Pro Vita Sua

Having summarized my bio,
I am now writing a poem
On the backside of a life
Typed full of errors.

Two sorts of summary show through.

My feelings are probably on edge like this
Page catches the purposeless breeze.

If I could,
I would
Slide out on the first wind.

I will, instead,
Try to sit still.

Hold myself up to the light like this.

A Needle's Eye

You'd think the children would believe,
But they have ever thought untrue
Stories that include 'do not.'
They are the least listened to.

I like to think those widened eyes
Are opened to admit a world,
But little wisdom always doubts
The truth in which it will be whirled.

My grandson grows incredulous
At my belief in darning flies:
That needles will knit up his lips
And stitch his lids down on his eyes.

I hate to think these simple tales
Are only true in adult lands,
That these fine threads are only felt
In tighter times, by older hands.

—1958

Central System

Everyone please note the frog
Like last week's dog
Is vertebrate
Is whole of spine
Is not yet dead

So naught will interfere
With the experiment
We amputate his brain
By the simple expedient
Of cutting off his head

There

Now hanging him from wire and fish hook
We take a bit of acid dipped white gauze
Apply it to his back
Note that in your note book without a pause
His hind leg reaches up to rub away
What he has never known since he was spawned
Beneath a log
In a green lily pond

Which proves the spine of any headless frog
Thus touched with sulphur brine
Though any acid serves
Connects directly to the

Nerves

To A Beauty

That ugly girl, who, seated by the wall,
Watches you moving at my side,
Has a better touch for distance,
Knowing your beauty through her pride.

Ignorant, you have been visited,
Toured like the rich palace of a king
Who never noticed, even as a child,
What could make some marvelling peasant sing.

Resort

Every summer they came,
Clapboard shingle and gull.
Wouldn't miss him,
Blind at the piano,
Still magic moving magic.

Husband died first she
Came twice after that.
Once soon after.
Once much later.
Years in between,
Clapboard shingle and gull,

And then there were none.

Tongues

Louis Tuleja could spit thick
Gobs of phlegm further
Than anyone in the gym
And with an aim so fine
He'd blot the brassy doorknob
You *were* about to turn

Or hang one from the ceiling
Right over your head
And you would cringe like Damocles
Calculating tensile strength
Or tonsil strength maybe

And Kookie Braniff's shoeshine shop
Had all its smokey windows
Stuffed with old green poolhall felt
To smother down
The drafts and weathers

He'd lounge mornings away
In his palace of dead air
Huffing mouthfuls slowly till
They settled over the fingers
Of dull black coathooks or the toes
Of upturned iron footrests

In those days a poet swore
His mouthings would be stable
On the page and in the mind
But age has blown him back to find
In cloudy word and line
This small personal triumph
Of a kind

Creative Writing Notebook: *Lesson No. 1*

Byron had a club foot.
He made love to his sister anyhow.
She was very beautiful
With many admirers.
She picked the brother with the club foot.

It is called swimming the Hellespont.

Milton liked the look of a king's head.
Off the body.
When in came the new king, he took a royal
Long look at Milton.
Milton stared back blindly.

It is called swimming the Hellespont.

Poets prove freedom by living it daily.
It is called swimming the Hellespont.
Anyone who can swim can be a poet.

Melodramatics

I

Curtains
Says the villain

Spotting consequence
Trammeling down the tracks

Foiled again

For heroes kisses
Thrown flowers
Champagnes
Big Party
Up at the armory

While shivering in his cape
Waiting the last freight
Out of this crummy town

Curtains
Says the villain
I simply tried to teach them

Style

II

Foiled
Does that mean

No more locomotives
No more hemp

Shall I do pushups
Get me a tan
Practise an open smile
A glad hand
Find a job
Work   uptoit   slow

After all
Nobody even looked at her
Never thought of her

That way

Was always Sis

Before

III

What is a poorboy to do
Other side of the tracks boy

Was it the threats?

But when she finds
It must be violent

What then Trueblood?

When she finds
I merely act your boyhood dreams

When she sees me
In your embarassed eyes

Admits to herself
She wanted me so many times

In the black of night

IV

There will be another time girl
Daddy finally gone

All of it yours at last
Far as you can see

There will be another time
By my filthiest oath

(*$&!*(—   (+&=)   /%$¢

I will lift your life from

Those frail hands

THE PROM: THREE POEMS

The Queen

Bats her eyes,
Flashes her green lids, she is
Drunk enough not to hope any longer
Others have drunk enough not to notice
She is taller than her partner.

Her bobbed hair bobs upon her bare shoulders.
It should be cut a bit but it grows so fast.
One can hardly keep up anymore.

The music is faster and her partner puffs.
He is also sweating, how does one say, profusely?
Her eyes shine again greeny like fireflies.

Is there no sweet black bird in the dark
To sight to soar to dip to take in beak
Her downy neck?

She would be Leda to a bat,
This poor Cleopatra,
Too tall for any serious love
And terrified of snakes.

Wallflower

What do they know, pretty and perfumed?
What if she can't dance, the boys wink anyway.

And later on when they are all tucked in
With teddybears and sugarplums and mother
Wets their forehead and turns out the light,
When the boys are at the diner drinking coffee,
Afraid to be the first one to go home,

She'll roll the blankets under from the right
And roll the blankets under from the left
And when she is cocooned up tight,
Warm as any butterfly,
She'll reach one tender finger down
And dance with all the handsome boys in town.

Chaperone

The crinoline outmodes him.
If he could
He'd stop the band, round up the girls,
Gather all the pinkness home.

Instead he drifts,
His hands remembering starch.

Why pick on him each dance?
He wears a bow tie and he smokes a pipe,
Is easy with the girls and jokes the boys.

He wishes that he would go bald,
Get paunchy, testy, be a principal.

He reaches all the way across the gym
To pull a junior's bodice higher.
Then he pulls it down again,
Kisses the nipples of her breasts,
Tears her underthings to shreds.
They couldn't stop him till he raped
Maybe even three.

He rubs his pipe against his nose
And the oil makes the grain come out.
His wife is knitting.
She looks up at him and smiles.

MOON POEMS

Projection

A bright moon can bring down the sky.
Tonight there is a bright moon, I
Have been brought down. Dark and low
Falls a foreshortened dim shadow.

If blackness has its shapes, those shapes
Are absences. But this one apes
My posture, queries all I've phrased
From life. I'm questioned. And I'm phased.

Wan, and in eclipse, I mock
The moon back, and begin to talk
Of differences face to face.
Moon men are a crusty race.

I quiz him how his fires died.
His craters argue that he tried.
Though guessing that he's deep and gold,
I kid about his hidden cold.

He asks me of my darker side.
I throw him shadows, and my hide
Obscures a more complete display.
I press him why he pales at day.

We'll be both finally found out,
Discovered down to the last doubt.
They'll learn his scars are spread the same
Over both sides. Though who's to blame?

And as for me, they'll learn that all
I would or could tell them, was all.
They won't believe one pockmarked page.
They'll say I lied about my Age.

—1962

The Tracks Of Tyros

With nothing more important up
Seven of us meet to spin
One Saturday afternoon away,
Guests of the government.

Somewhere in an atmosphere
Turned deep blue by the yellow sun,
A tiny eye at incredible speed
Watches our weathers.
Technicians perk their huge
Aluminum ears and wait.

They warm their brains up
And they wait. The time will tell.
The time will tell these circuits
When to think. They are searching
Our heavens.

We want to know what's up,
What's for us in the next few days:
Omens spelled out on a plastic strip
 (which stretches under too much strain).

We stand a little space apart.
One of the machines is red
And someone asks it for a Coke.
It doesn't laugh; it goes
About its father's business, scanning stars.

And we are told that in the future
 (which is very near)
This system will be totally unmanned.
The machines become excited.
The bird is overhead and squawks
Its message, and a miracle
Faithful to the hour
Shines to perfection. For a moment
We see ourselves
A moving map, a present globe.

Privileged, we peer at coasts
And clouds, we ponder boundaries,
We meditate from a point of view
A thousand statute miles from dizziness.

And then the little moon has set.
We pull on coats and fumble for our keys,
Ignite our cars and spin away
Over the same geographies
That we could not decipher minutes past.

The tracking station leaves our mirrors
Which only show the way we had arrived.

—1962

Moon Flight

Launch

He will become excited.
Within certain limits.
Then the elements will fume.

And with technicians numbering seconds
Like lovers
In some long drawn ponderous good-bye,
He will enter a silent heavy hesitance,
And then the timelessness of travel.

Some will turn away, others
Will follow him out of mind,
And a few will think, another

Emissary against dragons.

The Sea of Frigidity

Light, clumsy, breath
Coming upon demand,
He will stand
Upon the history
Of a million, upturned, night-torn eyes.

He will pick up a pebble of the moon.
It will be like the end of any love,
And he will stand,
Encratered, desolate,
Upon the stiffened shores of meteors,
The sharp horizon abruptly
Near, and a clouded future
Pendant in his sky.

Terminal

The thunder on the moon is silent.
It is no less there. Ask
Any of the moon's pedestrians.
He will smile the smile of

No one *you* know.
And then his lids will rise,
Like the doors on storm cellars,
And you will see emerge
The ancient look of the survivor,
Pupils wide with aftermath,
The mind's streets filled with leaves and litter,
Black homes,

And a snapped blue sparking.

—1963

BLUES IN BLACK AND WHITE

Down in the Ghetto

Big male chromosome comin down the street
Stop in front of the can dee store
Light his cee gar from the sole of one boot

He see the little girl chromosome
With the red dress on

She say dit dit dit

He say dah dah dah

She say again dit dit dit

Now that is my dominant strain chile
Your recessive too

S O S when I saw how
Hath God wrought you

Welfare Shout

She got high clear plastic heels
And red red lacquer on her toes,
Few blue veins back of her legs.
I love her just the same.

Two false teeth on the right side,
Big brass loop in one ear,
Always stands with one hand on her hip.
I love her just the same.

Brown love line down her belly,
Stretch marks either side,
She done a lot of romance,
I love her just the same.

Please, govermint, send me my check,
Hurry the mailman on.
But even if we both go thirsty,
I love her just the same.

Sharpy

Let me tell you this one thing
Before you go puttin on.

We all end up down and dirty.
You cant fight City Hall.

Beg among the pigeons,
Get you a fine statue,

Comes to the same thing buddy:
Down and dirty down down down

Down and dirty down

Owner

If I could sit here always,
Sun on my face,
Grass stem in my teeth,

Leanin here always,

But there's hay in the meadow,
Storm in the far sky.

If I could sit here always,
Sun on my face.

Dont it always happen dog?
Dont it   always happen.

Understanding Is A Tone Of Voice Blues

Our cat is so lazy
He get sore if you make him purr.

Why our cat is so lazy
You can pick him up,
Move him out,

Put him down.
He open one eye,
Tuck his left paw under his chin,
Open both eyes.
My, he say, it all different.

How I get heah?

Now that is lazy, mama.
But thats how
I make
Love.

Pick me up.
Move me out,
Put me down.

How I get heah?

And if you dont understand me,
I say *if* you dont understand me,
Well thats the

Understanding is a Tone of Voice

Blues.

Understanding Is A Tone Of Voice Blues Part Two

This is the flip side, brothers.
And sisters.

Said before our cat is lazy.
He fall asleep standin up.
Fall over like a bookend.
Or a doorstop.

Keep him anyway:
Props up books of poems.
Dont eat much,
Keeps the screen door tight,
Flies out.

And that's how
I make
Love:

Keep your door tight mama, hold
Your old book shelf.

How To Pick A Mistress, Or

Cat love the smell of my arm pit.
Nuzzle the nose up there like cat will.

Days I think
Last man on earth
No five day deodorant stick.

Patriotick.
Flags behind me when I walk.

And

Thinkin some cat I might meet,
Bathe each and every morning
Like sunwork.

So

If a big angel with a smug smile,
Flat on his back, rubbin his wings
In some big dusty bowl

Can be imagined,

Well that's me in my shower.
And this song is the flutter of the wings
On my guardian.

Heavenly. Even earthy,
Dust to dust speakin.

Pickanangelfeatherangelanyfeather,
My COY kitty.

A Writer's Attic

Moving is a kind of dying. One binds fast
As many ends and odds out of the past
As a sense of the ridiculous allows.
Some awkward items are too large, have lost
The magic of compelling an attachment.
The least important things are left for last.

Onetime sophisticate of the dining room,
That bureau of mahogany veneer,
Warped, and its one eye clouded over,
Used to frighten me with dark designs.
I wonder at its humbling. Mischief
Seems the new limit of imagination
And I can't think it cares for its demotion,
Though more than that is stolen by the years:
Books and clothing I grew out of, toys,
Some games, these could be handed down, although
Letters, photographs, newspaper clippings
Where I won a second or third prize,
I do not want to keep along. Or leave.
I carry bushels of them out as trash,
Mail them, in the fire, to the North Pole,
Which is the only spot I've ever heard
A hope to go to once it's spent in ink.
Or a fear even.

Enough of being childish.
A grown man couldn't help but snigger archly
If I let him overhear my musing.
With ease one must incinerate his trifles,
For who would have his pettiness revealed.
I carry bushels of it out as trash.
It is as if my bland objective eye
Won't understand. Or sympathize, perhaps.
I don't completely understand myself,
But at the aftertime of any loss,
There is deserves a pause of mind:
The what to take away, the what to leave behind.